# Solo and Duet Books

## *For the Piano*

**Collected and Harmonized,
Edited and Fingered
by ANGELA DILLER
and ELIZABETH QUAILE**

FIRST SOLO BOOK
*New Edition*

SECOND SOLO BOOK
*New Edition*

THIRD SOLO BOOK

FOURTH SOLO BOOK

FIRST DUET BOOK

SECOND DUET BOOK

THIRD DUET BOOK

# G. SCHIRMER, *Inc.*

DISTRIBUTED BY

HAL•LEONARD®
CORPORATION
7777 W. BLUEMOUND RD. P.O. BOX 13819 MILWAUKEE, WI 53213

ED. 2956

# FOREWORD TO THE 1974 REVISED EDITION

It seemed almost presumptuous to tamper with the First Solo Book which in its present form has meant so much to so many teachers and students. However, since a new edition became necessary, we agreed to prepare it because of our close association with the Diller-Quaile School of Music. In so doing we have been guided and helped by suggestions from our own faculty and many other teachers and students, and we are especially grateful to Mildred Bleier for the long hours she spent preparing the manuscript for the printer.

It has been our aim to change the book as little as possible. The main areas of change are:

1. Replacing most of the square brackets which indicated phrase structure by the more conventional slurs. In some cases the square brackets have been maintained but those below the left hand part have been moved above the treble staff so they could no longer be confused with pedal marks.

2. Adding words to many of the pieces in the hope that they will add to the interest of the pieces and help to clarify the phrasing.

3. Adding a few folk tunes from other Diller-Quaile sources in places where the music advanced too rapidly for some students.

4. Converting several of the one hand pieces to two hands.

We hope the book will continue its long and useful career in its new form.

> Dorothy Weed
> Teacher at the Diller-Quaile School of Music
> 1922 to the present
> Music Director 1955-1972
>
> Robert Fraley
> Teacher at the Diller-Quaile School of Music
> 1961 to the present
> Director since 1972

# PREFACE TO THE 1954 EDITION

## OBJECT OF THIS BOOK

The object of this book is to provide the student who is beginning piano lessons with material of permanent musical value. The pieces are arranged simply and pianistically. They are graded carefully, and new ideas are presented step by step.

The *First Solo Book* is appropriate for children who are starting lessons at the age of seven or eight. It can also be used successfully with Adult Beginners, because of the musical interest of the material. For students playing music of Grade Two, these pieces can be used for sight reading, or as pieces they learn alone.

Since this book is a collection of solo pieces, it is not primarily an Instruction Book, and can be used with any Method.

## CHOICE OF MATERIAL

With the exception of seven preparatory pieces, the music in the *First Solo Book* consists almost entirely of folk-tunes of many countries.

Folk music, because it has permanent musical value, is the best possible material for developing musical taste. It has stood the test of time. Tunes like "Sur le Pont d'Avignon" and "Frère Jacques" will probably be sung and played long after the "teaching pieces" that we write nowadays will have been forgotten. Nevertheless, these "teaching pieces" may well be used as supplementary material to folk music. Because of their wider compass on the keyboard, they are useful in developing pianism.

But folk music furnishes the soundest basis for the student's musical education. It leads easily and naturally to the Easy Classics, which in turn lead to the world's great piano literature.

## EXPLANATION OF THE EDITING OF THE PIECES

The pieces in the *First Solo Book* have been very carefully edited as to phrasing, touch, and dynamics. Since some of the details of printing are not in conventional style, the following brief explanation may be helpful to the student or teacher who uses this book.

### 1. Explanation of Signs

The slur ⌒ indicates *legato*; the dots ♩ ♩ ♩ indicate *staccato*; the slur and dots

♩ ♩ ♩ indicate *portato*. (Sometimes all three touches are used in the same piece, as, for

example, in No. 57, "In The Summer Time".) A note marked ♩ should receive special stress.

### 2. The Rhythmic Position of Dots

In this book, in the pieces where notes are followed by dots, the dots are not printed in the conventional place, next to the preceding notes. They are spaced so that the eye can see at once on which beat the dots occur rhythmically.

For example, in ¾ meter, a dot following a half note is printed in the last third of the measure,

because it represents the third beat ( | ♩ 1 2 3 • | not | ♩. 1 2 3 | ). See No. 3, "Up in the Sky".

Similarly, a dot following a quarter note is printed well to the right, so that the eye recognizes that the dot comes at the beginning of the following beat $\overset{1}{\downarrow}$ $\overset{2}{\bullet}$ ♪ not $\overset{1}{\downarrow}$. $\overset{2}{♪}$ ). See No. 24, "My Country, 'Tis of Thee".

For another example, see No. 54, "Pussy-Cat". In the third measure, the dots in the right hand are printed exactly above the third quarter note in the left hand, with which they agree rhythmically.

## 3. $\frac{6}{8}$ Meter

In the first eight pieces in $\frac{6}{8}$ meter, beginning with No. 29, two meter signs are given: the conventional $\frac{6}{8}$, followed by $\left( \overset{2}{\downarrow}. \right)$. This is to remind the student that some pieces in $\frac{6}{8}$ meter are counted with six beats in the measure (one beat for each eighth), and others are counted with two beats to the measure (one beat for each dotted quarter). Whether you count six beats or two beats to the measure depends, of course, on the speed of the piece.

In the pieces after No. 46, however, only the conventional $\frac{6}{8}$ sign is used.

## 4. Phrase Lengths

Since phrases frequently do not end at the bar-line, this fact has been taken into account in the printing of this book. For example, in No. 27, "The Vicar of Bray", the melody begins on the fourth beat, the phrases end on the third beat, and the count of the piece is "Four-*One*-Two-Three". The measure at the end of the line is left open on the third beat, and the fourth beat is printed at the beginning of the next line, where the new phrase begins.

This device of printing is used in similar cases throughout the book, and will help the student to read intelligently in phrase lengths, and not by the measure from bar-line to bar-line.

## 5. Fingering

Fingering is given at the beginning of phrases and at a shift in hand position. But obvious fingering, such as in passages along the scale line or chord line, is not usually printed. A repeated note, unless otherwise indicated, is played with the same finger.

The accurate observance of indicated fingering is an important part of sight reading. Therefore, if you do not wish a student to use the fingering that is printed, by all means cancel the printed fingering and write in your own. For example, if a 4 is printed over a note, and the student is to use 3, cross out the 4 and write in the 3, so that the student will not acquire the very bad habit of looking at printed fingering, but not following it. It is important that his eye be correlated with his sense of touch.

## THE VALUE OF ENSEMBLE PLAYING

Ensemble playing is a delightful way of stimulating the student's musical awareness. Two books in this category were written specifically to be used in conjunction with the *First Solo Book*. They are the *First Duet Book* and *Second Piano Parts to First Solo Book Pieces*.

The *First Duet Book* is a collection of pieces for teacher and pupil to play 4-hands at one piano. The introduction of new material follows in general the plan of the *First Solo Book*.

The *Second Piano Parts* are an enlargement of the musical content of the pieces in the *First Solo Book*. They are written in a variety of styles: some are contrapuntal, some furnish chord background, and some are more elaborate accompaniments. But they are all written in a style suggested by the folk-tunes themselves. These two-piano pieces make a pleasant diversion and will give variety to a Pupils' Recital. The student can play the solo alone, and immediately repeat it, with the second piano part added by another student or by the teacher.

# SUGGESTIONS FOR TEACHING FIRST GRADE MATERIAL

The following suggestions may be helpful to teachers in using this book or any similar material with their students.

### 1. Singing while playing the melodic line

While he plays, the child can sing the tune, identifying in turn: 1) time-values, 2) the count, 3) the letter-names of the notes, and 4) the numbers of the fingers he is using. The tune should be played at the same speed at each repetition.

For example, No. 26, "All the Birds Have Come Again", could be sung as in the following illustration:

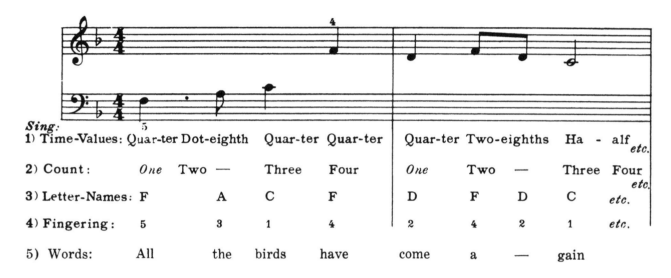

| Sing: | | | | | | | | | |
|---|---|---|---|---|---|---|---|---|---|
| 1) Time-Values: | Quar-ter | Dot-eighth | Quar-ter | Quar-ter | Quar-ter | Two-eighths | Ha | - | alf *etc.* |
| 2) Count: | *One* | Two — | Three | Four | *One* | Two — | | Three | Four *etc.* |
| 3) Letter-Names: | F | A | C | F | D | F | D | C | *etc.* |
| 4) Fingering: | 5 | 3 | 1 | 4 | 2 | 4 | 2 | 1 | *etc.* |
| 5) Words: | All | the | birds | have | come | a | — | gain | |

Singing while playing, as given in the above illustration, will bring variety to a child's practicing. He will have to keep his eyes on the notes, instead of looking down at his hands, and through this, the teacher can be sure that the child understands what he sees on the printed page.

### 2. Looking over the piece as a whole

Before a student begins to play a piece, he should look over the music to discover all that he can about it, and to be sure that he understands the printed indications such as the key signature, time-values, the count, indications of touch, dynamics, and phrasing, and the meaning of such words as *andante, legato, a tempo,* etc. if these occur in the piece.

The teacher should also help him to discover, in the printed music, something of the structure of the piece, such as repetitions, sequences, chords, phrase lengths, etc. The amount of "information" you will discuss depends entirely on the age and musical maturity of the student. A child will be able to recognize only the most elementary things, but an older student will probably be interested in making a more detailed analysis of the musical structure of the pieces he plays.

For example, if a child is to learn No. 74, "Russian Cradle-Song":

## Russian Cradle-Song

he should be able, using his own words, to describe the piece as follows. The teacher may help him by asking him leading questions.

"This is a Russian Cradle-Song. The key signature of one flat shows two keys, either F major or D minor. (You do not have to look at the last note of a piece to discover whether it is in major or minor! It *begins* in the key in which it is written, and the Tonic chord usually appears in the first two or three measures.) The notes D F A appear in the first measure, showing that the piece is in D minor.

The meter is Two-Four; the count *One*-Two. Time-values are eighth notes, quarters, and half notes. In the fourth measure half notes and quarters are heard together.

The slurs mean that the piece is played legato throughout, although the last note is staccato. *Andante* means going slowly, *p* stands for

*piano* and means soft, ![crescendo hairpin] means growing louder, *mf* stands for

*mezzo forte* and means half loud, *dim.* stands for *diminuendo* and means growing softer, and *pp* means *pianissimo*, twice as soft as *piano*.

The fingers the piece starts with are Left hand 5 on F, Right hand 4 on D.

The piece is made of two four-measure groups. In the first group, the first and second measures are the same. The first two measures in the second group are almost the same. The third and fourth measures of each group are different."

An older student might be interested to discuss the form in greater detail, as follows:

"The phrasing in the first group follows the familiar pattern, one measure plus one measure plus two measures $(1 + 1 + 2)$. In the first two measures the melody in the right hand moves downward in contrary motion to the rising bass. In the third and fourth measures the melody swings up the scale to A, heading for the half cadence on the Dominant triad, A major. A suspension in the left hand heightens the harmonic interest.

The phrasing in the second group, as in the first, is one measure plus one, plus two. The first measure begins with A in the right hand and F in the left. In the second measure, these notes are reversed: F is in the right hand, and A in the left. In the last two measures, the melody swings down to the tonic, D, in contrast to the corresponding measures of the first group. The tune is topped off by a final rising octave D to D. The cadence chords are $I_6^4$ $V^7$ I.

The tune is made of a combination of chord tones and non-harmonic tones. (It is interesting to hear the harmonic outline of the melody, indicated by the notes that are circled in the printed music above. These notes played in succession form a basic melody in quarter notes.)"

The more the student recognizes by looking over a piece as a whole before he begins to play, the more intelligent will be his practicing. All of these details of structure are to be listened to in playing. The more the student recognizes the relationship of the different parts of a piece, the more interesting his playing will be, both for himself and his hearers.

The notes of any piece can be played "correctly" and in time, but may still not give any idea of its musical content.

The "Russian Cradle-Song" is a poetic little piece, and should be played with sensitive understanding.

### 3. Practicing parallel passages

Passages of identical or similar construction occur in most music. Many folk-tunes contain phrases that are repeated identically as far as the notes are concerned, but may, in the repetition, have a different musical meaning, if the dynamics and touch are varied. This book has been particularly carefully edited as to dynamic marks and touch indications in these repeated passages.

Examine, for example, the following illustration of the German folk-tune, "In Springtime".

# In Springtime

Allegro

German Folk-Tune

The melody of three of the four sections is identical. These three sections, one in the bass, two in the treble, are marked Ⓐ . But although the melody is the same, the markings of touch and dynamics are quite different in each repetition.

On its first appearance, the tune, here in the left hand, begins *mf*, and there is a *crescendo* to the end; the third measure is played *portato*. The second appearance follows at once in the right hand, and this time the last two measures are harmonized. It starts *piano* and a *crescendo* and *diminuendo* extend over the last four measures, which are played *legato* throughout. At the last repetition, the tune is again in the right hand, but here begins *mf* with a two-measure *crescendo*. There is a sudden drop to a *piano* ending in the last two measures.

If these markings of dynamics and touch are observed, the meaning of the three passages will be different. It is somewhat like speaking a sentence in English, and inflecting it in different ways. Each inflection will carry a different meaning.

An excellent way for a student to hear these differences in musical "inflection" is for him to play parallel and similar passages out of context. In studying "In Springtime", for example, the student should play in succession the first two measures of each of the three Ⓐ sections, observing carefully the dynamic markings, and listening to the contrast in tone. Then he should play the last two measures of each Ⓐ section, comparing them also "by ear". Next he should play the complete four-measure sections in succession.

The student will now have a clear idea of the differences in meaning of the *three* sections. When

VIII

he plays the piece as a whole, it will have gained greatly in musical interest to him, and his musical hearing will have been infinitely sharpened. If, instead, he had confined his study to playing the piece straight through from beginning to end, it is probable that his ear would not have realized accurately the dynamic changes in the repeated passages.

Practicing parallel passages and phrases in this way is recommended for studying all music. It is an excellent way of keeping the mind alert and the ear active.

---

The value of this book lies, of course, in the musical quality of the pieces themselves. They offer a variety of musical experience: some are familiar songs, some are dances, some are lyrical, some are amusing, and so on. There is also variety of musical structure, such as irregular phrase lengths, sequences, modulations, etc. The editors have been guided in their suggestions of interpretation by the inherent content of the music itself.

---

Thanks are due to Thomas Whitney Surette, who suggested in 1917 that Elizabeth Quaile and I should write a beginner's piano book based on folk-tunes.

The *First Solo Book* and the *First Duet Book* were published in 1918, and became the first volumes in the Diller-Quaile Series.

After all these years, a new edition of the *First Solo Book* was necessary. Since the death of Miss Quaile in 1951, I have hesitated to make any revision of the book that we had written together. But now I have undertaken the task, although the work had to be done without the collaboration and counsel of my dear friend.

ANGELA DILLER

New York City
Spring, 1954

# INDEX OF TITLES

|  |  | Page |
|---|---|---|
| ALL THE BIRDS HAVE COME AGAIN | German | 8 |
| AUTUMN SONG | Slavonic | 14 |
| BAA, BAA, BLACK SHEEP | | 2 |
| BASQUE AIR | Spanish | 24 |
| BERCEUSE | French | 26 |
| BOHEMIAN MELODY | Bohemian | 7 |
| BOHEMIAN SONG | Bohemian | 5 |
| BRING A TORCH, JEANETTE, ISABELLA | French | 27 |
| CHRISTMAS SONG | German | 15 |
| COCK-A-DOODLE-DOO! | English | 31 |
| CRADLE-SONG | French | 18 |
| DAME, GET UP AND BAKE YOUR PIES | English | 16 |
| DISAGREEABLE LOVER, THE | Russian | 6 |
| EARLY ONE MORNING | English | 35 |
| EVENING | German | 7 |
| FOLK-SONG | German | 25 |
| FRÈRE JACQUES | French | 17 |
| FUN, FUN! | | 1 |
| GATHERING MUSSELS | French | 22 |
| GERMAN CRADLE SONG | German | 30 |
| GOING TO THE FAIR | Irish | 28 |
| HARLEQUIN | | 3 |
| HIPPITY HOP! | English | 15 |
| HOP, HOP, HOP | German | 9 |
| HOT CROSS BUNS | | 3 |
| HOW SHOULD I YOUR TRUE LOVE KNOW | English | 21 |
| HUNTING SONG | French | 19 |
| HUSH-A-BY BABY | | 2 |
| IF ALL THE WORLD WERE PAPER | | 12 |
| IF I WERE A NIGHTINGALE | English | 6 |
| IN SPRINGTIME | German | 25 |
| IN THE SUMMER TIME | French | 21 |
| IRISH TUNE | Irish | 16 |
| JACK, BE NIMBLE | | 3 |
| JIG | French | 18 |
| KEYS OF CANTERBURY, THE | English | 30 |
| LAMENT | Moravian | 33 |
| LAVENDER'S BLUE | English | 29 |
| LITTLE BO-PEEP | J. M. Elliot | 16 |
| LITTLE JACK HORNER | | 6 |
| LOOK AT THE BEAR | | 17 |
| LULLABY | Bohemian | 24 |
| MAN WITH THE BAGPIPES, THE | French | 29 |
| MARCHING SONG | | 4 |
| MELODY | French | 23 |
| MINOR SCALES (Natural, Harmonic, Melodic) | | 14 |
| MORNING SONG | French | 34 |
| MY COUNTRY, 'TIS OF THEE | | 7 |
| NIGHTINGALE, THE | German | 22 |
| NORTHERN SONG | Russian | 18 |
| O! LITTLE JACK SPRATT | English | 35 |
| ODD OR EVEN | | 12 |
| ODD OR EVEN (Second Arrangement) | | 12 |
| ODD OR EVEN (Third Arrangement) | | 12 |
| OLD CHATEAU, THE | French | 32 |
| OVER THE MEADOW | Lithuanian | 5 |
| PIERROT | French | 4 |

| | | | |
|---|---|---|---|
| PLANTING THE CABBAGE | | *French* | 28 |
| PUSSY-CAT | | *English* | 19 |
| RAINDROPS | | *Bohemian* | 20 |
| RHYTHMIC STUDIES (3) | | | 13 |
| RIDE A COCK-HORSE | | | 2 |
| RIGGITY JIG | | | 10 |
| RIGGITY JIG (Second Arrangement) | | | 11 |
| RIGGITY JIG (Third Arrangement) | | | 11 |
| RIGGITY JIG (Fourth Arrangement) | | | 11 |
| RUSSIAN CRADLE-SONG | | *Russian* | 28 |
| RUSTIC SONG | | *Dutch* | 22 |
| SHEPHERDESS, THE | | *Russian* | 34 |
| SING A SONG O' SIXPENCE | | | 5 |
| SING, SING | | | 1 |
| SISTER ANN | | | 1 |
| SKIPPING | | *French* | 15 |
| SLUMBER-SONG | | *Bohemian* | 8 |
| SONG OF THE SWORD | | | 17 |
| STAR OF THE SEA | | *French* | 32 |
| STUDY IN F | | | 7 |
| STUDY IN G | | | 3 |
| SUR LE PONT D'AVIGNON | | *French* | 4 |
| SUSA, LITTLE SUSA | | *German* | 23 |
| THERE WAS A MAID WENT TO THE MILL | | *English* | 13 |
| TOWN CLOCK, THE | | *Weckerlin* | 20 |
| TRAMP, TRAMP, TRAMPING | | *English* | 21 |
| UP IN THE SKY | | | 1 |
| VESPER SONG | | *French* | 31 |
| VICAR OF BRAY, THE | | *English* | 9 |
| WALTZ | | *Moravian* | 26 |

"Collected and Arranged by Angela Diller and Elizabeth Quaile"

# First Solo Book

## Fun, Fun!

1. Fun, fun! Oh, what fun! Mu - sic les - sons have be - gun!

## Sister Ann

2. Ann, Ann, sis - ter Ann, Al - ways plays the best she can.

## Up in the Sky

3. Up in the sky, ev - er so high, Sky-larks are sing - ing as home-ward they fly.

## Sing, Sing

4. Sing, sing, what shall I sing? The cat's run a - way with the pud-ding-bag string.

47304c

## Ride a Cock-Horse

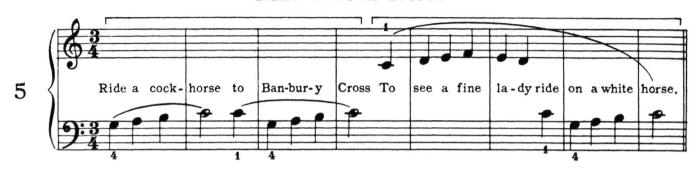

5

Ride a cock-horse to Ban-bur-y Cross To see a fine la-dy ride on a white horse.

## Hush-a-by Baby

6

Hush - a - by Ba - by, Thy cra - dle is green, Fa - ther's a no - ble - man, Moth - er's a queen; And Bet - ty's a la - dy And wears a gold ring, And John-nie's a drum-mer and drums for the queen.

## Baa, Baa, Black Sheep

7

"Baa, baa, black sheep, have you an-y wool?" "Yes, Sir, yes, Sir, three bags full."

## Harlequin

## Jack, be Nimble

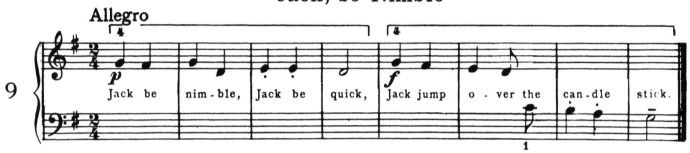

## Hot Cross Buns

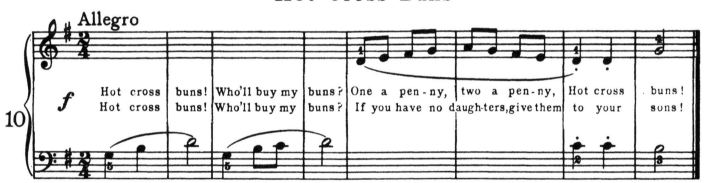

## Study in G

4

## Marching Song

12

## Pierrot

French Folk-Tune

13

"In the sil-ver moon-light, Oh Pier-rot my friend, I would now a word write Thy pen kind-ly lend!
"In the sil-ver moon-light," Pier-rot cross-ly said: "I've no pen for writ-ing, I am in my bed.

Can-dle-light has van-ished and no fire I see; O-pen wide the door, then, If you care for me."
Go and see my neigh-bor, she is there at home, Po-king up the fire-wood, keep-ing snug and warm."

## Sur le Pont d'Avignon

French Folk-Tune

14

On the bridge A-vign-on, All are danc-ing, All are dancing, On the bridge Avign-on, All are dancing in a ring

47304

# Sing a Song o' Sixpence

Sing a song o' six-pence, a pock-et full o' rye, Four and twenty blackbirds baked in a pie.

When the pie was o-pened the birds be-gan to sing. Was-n't that a dain-ty dish to set be-fore the king?

# Bohemian Song

# Over the Meadow

Lithuanian Folk-Tune

## The Disagreeable Lover

Russian Folk-Tune

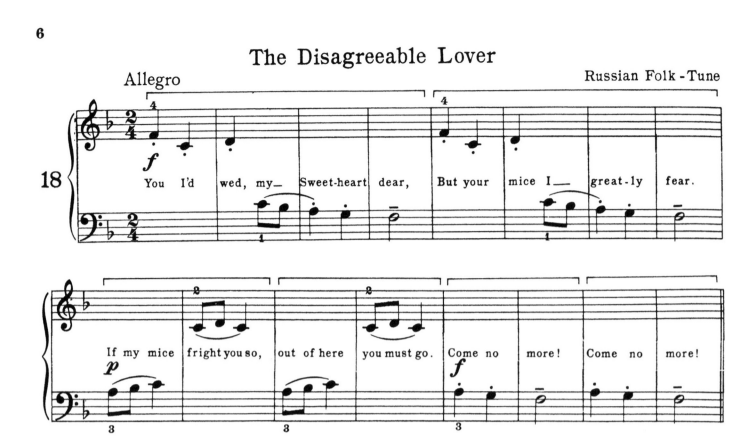

18

You I'd wed, my Sweet-heart dear, But your mice I greatly fear.

If my mice fright you so, out of here you must go. Come no more! Come no more!

## Little Jack Horner

Allegretto

19

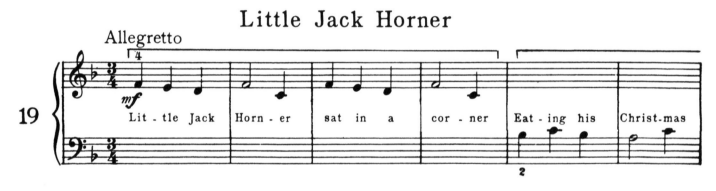

Lit - tle Jack Horn - er sat in a cor - ner Eat - ing his Christ-mas

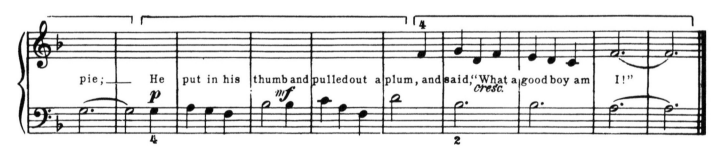

pie;— He put in his thumb and pulled out a plum, and said, "What a good boy am I!"

## If I Were a Nightingale

Allegro

English Folk-Tune

20

## Study in F

## Bohemian Melody

## Evening

German Folk-Tune

## My Country, 'tis of Thee

(optional)

47304

8

## Slumber-Song

2Bohemian Folk-Tune

## All the Birds Have Come Again

German Folk-Tune

47304

# The Vicar of Bray

Maestoso

Old English Tune

# Hop, Hop, Hop

Allegretto

German Folk-Tune

Hop, Hop, Hop! Nim-ble as a top. Po-ny, you must trav-el fast-er

If you want to please your mas-ter. Hop,Hop,Hop,Hop, Hop! Nim-ble as a top.

The next pieces are in a new meter, $\frac{6}{8}$ (six-eight). You count *two* in each measure, just as in two-four meter, but here each of the two counts is divided into *three* eighth-notes. That is why they use this peculiar meter-sign,—to account for all of the eighth-notes. But it really sounds like two counts in the measure. To make the arithmetic look right, each undivided beat is printed with a quarter-note and a dot ($\text{\musQuarter}$), so the meter-sign might be $\frac{6}{8} = \frac{2}{\text{\musDotQuarter}}$.

# Riggity Jig

The first piece, "Riggity Jig," is printed in four different arrangements.

In the first arrangement, you have to play only the notes that come at the *beginning* of each beat.

In the second arrangement, some of the beats are "decorated" with three eighth-notes.

In the third arrangement, more beats are decorated.

And in the fourth arrangement, the tune is printed as it really is, with all the decorations.

You will not be playing enough notes to fit all the words till you come to the fourth arrangement.

Try to play all four arrangements at the same speed.

First Arrangement.

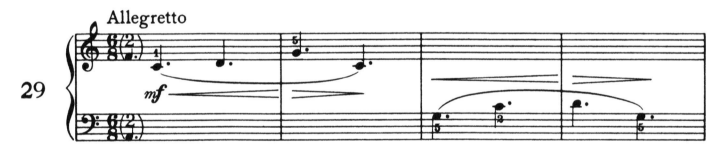

*To the Teacher:* The method of study on these two pages, using rhythmic and harmonic analysis, is, of course, the basis of all rote teaching. The student should be helped to *study all of his pieces* in this way, before he begins to *practice* them.

Second Arrangement.

30

Third Arrangement.

31

Fourth Arrangement.

32

Rig - gi - ty jig, and a - way we will go, Rig-gi-ty jig to the cir - cus!

Ca-mels and el - e-phants all in a row, Rig-gi-ty jig to the cir - cus!

47304

Here is another piece in $\frac{6}{8}$ meter, printed in three arrangements—one plain, and two decorated. The words fit the third arrangement, which is the real tune.

## Odd or Even

First Arrangement.

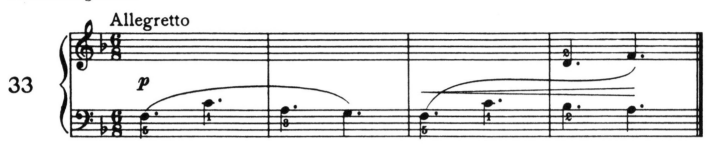

Second Arrangement.

Third Arrangement.

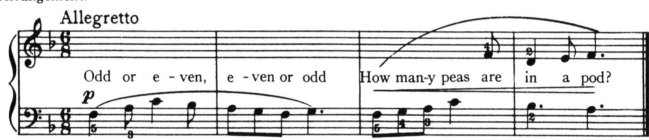

## If all the World were Paper

English Folk-Tune

## Rhythmic Study

## Rhythmic Study

## Rhythmic Study

## There was a Maid Went to the Mill

English Folk-Tune

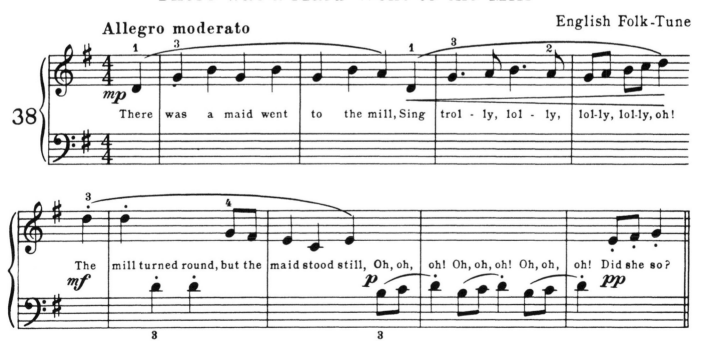

There was a maid went to the mill, Sing trol - ly, lol - ly, lol-ly, lol-ly, oh!

The mill turned round, but the maid stood still, Oh, oh, oh! Oh, oh, oh! Oh, oh, oh! Did she so?

# Natural, Harmonic, and Melodic Minor

## Autumn Song

Slavonic Folk-Tune

## Skipping

French Folk-Tune

**41**

## Hippity Hop!

English Folk-Tune

**42**

Hip-pi-ty hop to the bar-ber shop To buy a stick of can-dy.

One for you and one for me, But none for sis-ter Man-dy!

## Christmas Song

German Folk-Tune

**43**

47304

16

## Irish Tune

## Dame, Get Up and Bake Your Pies

## Little Bo-peep

47304

## Look at the Bear

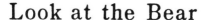

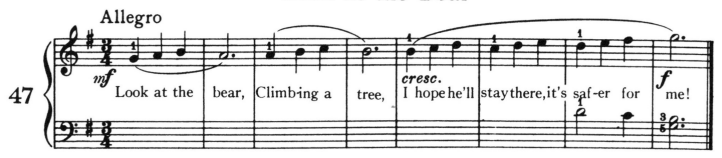

## Frère Jacques

FRENCH FOLK-TUNE

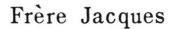

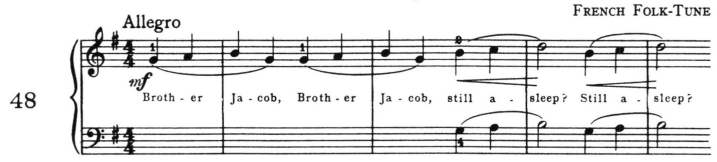

## Song of the Sword

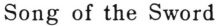

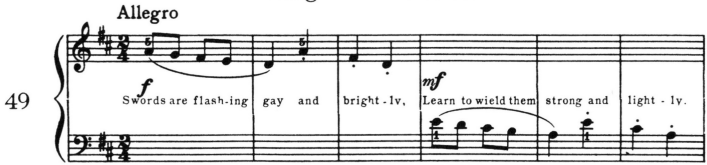

47304

# Jig

# Hunting Song

French Folk-Tune

# Pussy-Cat

English Folk-Tune

# The Town Clock

Raindrops

# In the Summer Time

French Folk-Tune, Adapted

# How Should I Your True Love Know

English Folk-Tune

# Tramp, Tramp, Tramping

English Folk-Tune

22

Gathering Mussels

Rustic Song

The Nightingale

47304

# Melody

French Folk-Tune

## Susa, Little Susa

German Folk-Tune

Su - sa, lit-tle Su - sa, what stirs in the hay? The geese are go-ing

bare - foot the whole live-long day. The cob - bler has leath - er, his

last he did lose; And so the lit - tle gos-lings must go with - out shoes.

# Basque Air

Spanish Folk-Tune

## Lullaby

Bohemian Folk-Tune

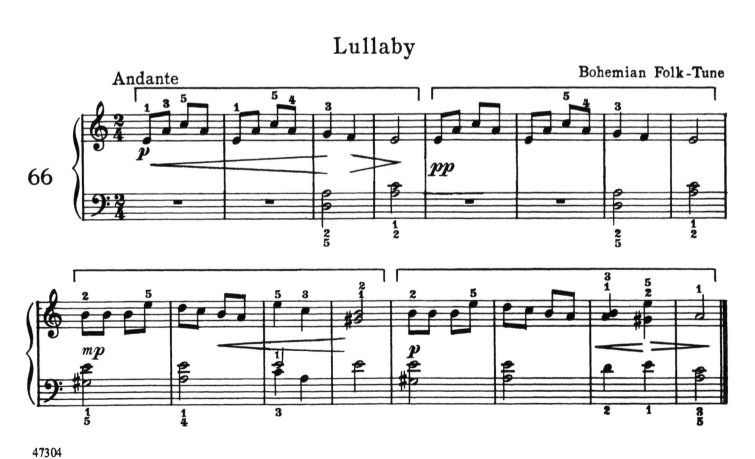

## Folk-Song

German Folk-Tune

## In Springtime

German Folk-Tune

## Berceuse

Andante

French Folk-Tune

69

## Waltz

Allegretto

Moravian Folk-Tune

70

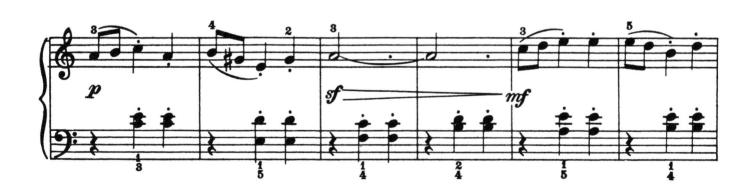

## Bring a Torch, Jeanette, Isabella

Andantino

Old French Carol

71

*mp* Bring a torch,— Jean - nette, Is - a - bel - la, Bring a torch,— and

quick - ly run. *mf* Christ is born,— good folk of the vil - lage,

*p* Christ— is born and Mar - y's call - ing, *p* Ah! Ah!

Beau - ti - ful is the Moth - er, Ah! *pp* Ah! Beau - ti - ful is her Son.

# Going to the Fair

Allegretto

Irish Folk-Tune

72

# Planting the Cabbage

Allegro

French Folk-Tune

73

Plant the cab-bage seeds to - day, Here's the way, here's the way.

Plant the cab-bage seeds to - day, Now it's work and now it's play.

# Russian Cradle-Song

Andante

74

# The Man with the Bagpipes

## Lavender's Blue

30

# The Keys of Canterbury

# German Cradle Song

47304

# Vesper Song

French Folk-Tune

# Cock-a-doodle-doo!

English Folk-Tune

Cock-a-doo-dle- doo! My dame has lost her shoe. My master's lost his fiddling stick don't know what to do.

## Star of the Sea

French Folk-Tune

**81**

## The Old Chateau

French Folk-Tune

**82**

# Lament

47304

# Morning Song

French Folk-Tune

# The Shepherdess

Russian Folk-Tune

## O! Little Jack Spratt

English Folk-Tune

## Early One Morning

English Folk-Tune

# ANALYTICAL INDEX

(The following index is a sort of "work-sheet" such as Miss Quaile and I prepared when writing this book. It is concerned entirely with what the student must learn to read. The different elements of structure, such as repetitions, modulations, irregular phrase lengths, etc., are introduced in a carefully planned order throughout the book, but are not indicated in this index.)

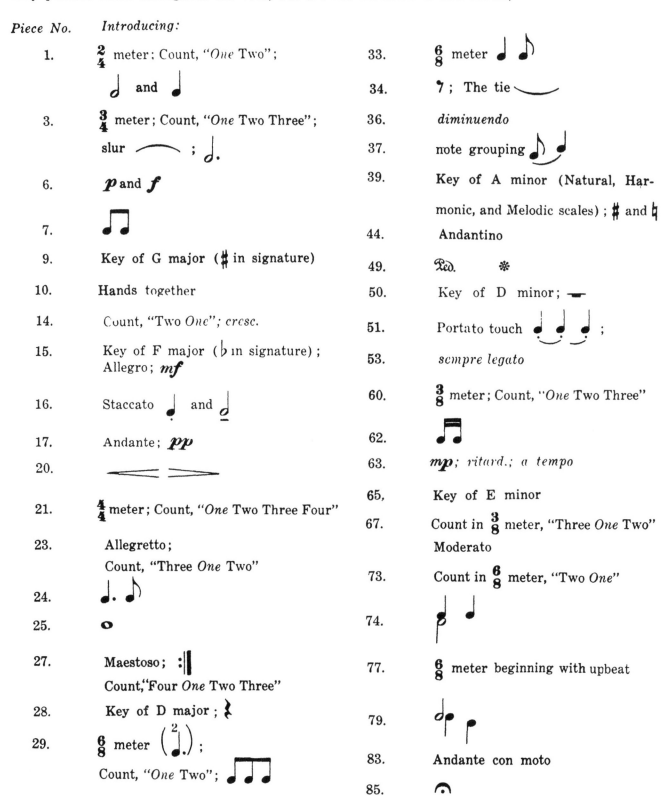

Piece No.   Introducing:

1.   ²⁄₄ meter; Count, "One Two"; ♩ and ♩

3.   ³⁄₄ meter; Count, "One Two Three"; slur ⌣ ; ♩.

6.   *p* and *f*

7.   ♫

9.   Key of G major (♯ in signature)

10.   Hands together

14.   Count, "Two One"; *cresc.*

15.   Key of F major (♭ in signature); Allegro; *mf*

16.   Staccato ♩ and ♩

17.   Andante; *pp*

20.   ⟨ ⟩

21.   ⁴⁄₄ meter; Count, "One Two Three Four"

23.   Allegretto; Count, "Three One Two"

24.   ♩. ♪

25.   𝅝

27.   Maestoso; :‖ Count, "Four One Two Three"

28.   Key of D major; 𝄾

29.   ⁶⁄₈ meter (♩.); Count, "One Two"; ♫♪

33.   ⁶⁄₈ meter ♩ ♪

34.   𝄿 ; The tie ⌣

36.   *diminuendo*

37.   note grouping ♪ ♩

39.   Key of A minor (Natural, Harmonic, and Melodic scales) ; ♯ and ♮

44.   Andantino

49.   𝄐 ❋

50.   Key of D minor; ―

51.   Portato touch ♩ ♩ ♩ ;

53.   *sempre legato*

60.   ³⁄₈ meter; Count, "One Two Three"

62.   ♫

63.   *mp*; *ritard.*; *a tempo*

65,   Key of E minor

67.   Count in ³⁄₈ meter, "Three One Two" Moderato

73.   Count in ⁶⁄₈ meter, "Two One"

74.   ♩ ♩

77.   ⁶⁄₈ meter beginning with upbeat

79.   ♩ ♩

83.   Andante con moto

85.   𝄐